THE BEST BOOK ON HOW TO MAKE MONEY ONLINE: a step-by-step guide

by Zackary Richards

Ari Publishing

This book is dedicated to all the hard working people lost their jobs during the financial meltdown

Disclaimer

NOTE* The author makes no guarantees that you will make any money using the methods outlined in this book. Success in ANY business depends on many factors including hard work and a bit of luck.

That being said, a considerable amount of money HAS been made by people using the processes outlined in the following chapters.

As an author, marketer and entrepreneur, the author has installed several links to sites that, in addition to providing online money making products, carry other products as well and should you purchase them the author may receive a commission.

Where to Begin

Did you know that Vic Strizheus made a record $710,000 online in ONE MONTH?

Or that Alex Becker, made over 2 million online last year and is positioned to make 3 million this year?

Or that Greg Morrison, Mike Long and the OMG (One Man Gang) team make over one million dollars a month online?

Did you know none of these people manufactured a single product? Haven't written a single book, or a line of computer code? Haven't built a huge internet business like Amazon?

In fact, most of them only work a few hours a day.

Yet they have become rich

<u>Very Rich!</u>

So how did they and **<u>thousands of others</u>** make so much money online?

Simple. They saw the many opportunities making money online provides and decided that was something they were going to do.

You can too.

And if you ask anyone of them what special talents or abilities they possess that made such success possible, they will tell you that they don't have any "Special talents" or "abilities". In fact once you get to know them you realize pretty quickly that they are just regular people—not much different from you and me.

But they must have had some advantage, some special trick that made it possible for them to have done so well.

Right?

Nope. But they all realized one thing. And it was Alex Becker of http://source-wave.com who pointed out the most important factor when it comes to making money and that is:

In Order to Make Money, You Have to Increase Your

Knowledge on <u>HOW</u> to Make Money.

It's that simple. Understanding <u>HOW</u> to make money comes <u>BEFORE</u> making money.

You don't attempt to start a Wal-Mart size business if you don't yet have the skills to run a successful hot-dog stand.

So how do you get that knowledge? I'm going to teach it to you. And where did I get that knowledge? I got it from successful online marketers who simply decided that they no longer wanted to spend their lives working hard to make someone else rich. If they were going to work hard anyway, then why not do it to make themselves rich?

And so they did.

So can you. And we're going to start right now

Since there is no way for me to know how much or how little experience you have making money online, I can't fine tune this guide to skip over the parts you might already know and get right to the part that puts money in your pocket.

But let me first point out that making money online is NO get-rich-quick scheme.

Making money online IS the future and I'll explain why you absolutely need to start doing it NOW a little later on in the book.

One of the first lessons is the importance of "Filling a Need". I wrote this book because many people are having a hard time getting a good job or getting one that pays a decent salary. And that's not their fault, many jobs have been eliminated due to advances in technology.

And this WILL continue. Over the next decade the majority of jobs that require human skills or physicality will be likely cut in half.

Here's are the FACTS:

As I write this book the stock market is at its highest point EVER. Major corporations and Wall Street are making record profits, and paying HUGE bonuses.

So, if American business is doing so well, why is there still high unemployment?

It's because the American worker is being phased out!

Business is evolving. The big box brick and mortar stores are in decline. You've no doubt heard about the problems Sears, K-Mart & JC Penny are having and even Walmart, the biggest of them all is experiencing decreasing profits.

Small Mom & Pop stores are disappearing and brick & mortar start-ups are failing at a frightening rate.

Why?

The Internet. Shopping on the internet has irrevocably changed the way we do business. In addition, more people are purchasing products from internet businesses every year and the trend is likely to continue.

Need an example? Look at Amazon. It has no Brick & Mortar stores, no sales people, no cleaning crews, no payments to ASCAP, no 'wet floor' lawsuits, no display windows, no holiday decorations, etc.

The only thing it does is present products at a far lower cost, delivers it with a day or so and has a 'no questions asked' return policy.

And although the company has no sales people, Amazon has won the #1 spot for customer satisfaction for nine years in a row!

So why on earth would a potential businessperson looking to start their own business, lay out a large amount of money (and place themselves in considerable debt) to open a physical store when that store will likely become a showplace for Amazon's products and sell no products of its own.

That's what happened to the bookstores and why they're disappearing. People enter a book store, peruse the shelves, select a book, take a seat in one of the comfy chairs the book stores offer and start reading.

They discover they like it and are going to buy it. But do they buy it from the bookstore? Of course not, the bookstore charges suggested retail. Instead they go home, hop on line and buy the same book on Amazon for a third of the price.

And this practice does only apply to book stores.

A few months ago my sister's driver's side window open/close control shorted out. She brought her car to two different repair shops and was quoted the repair price of $235 & $260 respectively.

So instead of laying out that kind of money, she snapped open the window panel, popped the chip and looked it up on Amazon.

She found it and the price was $40. So she ordered it, it arrived two days later, she snapped in the new one and the window was once again working properly.

The Walmart in my area recently increased the number of self-checkout lanes from four to twelve. The local big-box supermarkets quickly followed suit.

Recently on Jeopardy, IBM rolled out a computer named WATSON and claimed it could answer the spoken Jeopardy questions more accurately and faster than Ken Jennings and Brad Rutter, the game's two best contestants and biggest winners.

The competition was held over three games. At the end WATSON had trounced them both leading Ken Jennings to say, *"I, for one, welcome out new computer overlords."*

Those words, although spoken in jest, are quickly becoming a frightening truth.

You realize that IBM didn't spend millions of dollars and man hours simply to create a device that could win at Jeopardy, although that is what they want you to think.

Watson's real purpose is to replace ALL the customer service employees in all countries. And why not? It can answer any customer question better and faster than any human employee. It doesn't sleep, or take lunch breaks or holidays. It doesn't get sick, it doesn't need medical coverage, a 401K, life insurance or maternity leave.

So if you so happen to work in customer service or a similar job, you REALLY NEED THIS BOOK.

So what jobs are safe?

If you're considering going into the field of medicine and taking on an enormous amount of student loan debt that CAN'T be erased by filing bankruptcy, you should know that MRI scanners are becoming remarkably efficient and are rapidly approaching the point where not only will they be able to find and identify every possible illness, they will, like WATSON, have IMMEDIATE access to EVERY possible successful treatment.

And should you consider becoming a surgeon keep in mind that robotic surgeries are already commonplace and are being used in such complicated procedures as cancer removal and heart repair.

How about a career in Accounting?

You've heard of Turbo-tax and Quick books haven't you? How long do you think it will take before more advanced software programs eliminate the need for someone to do your books? People don't like strangers knowing their business so when the opportunity arises, most will chose software over an actual person.

Architecture?

Think about it. Millions of dollars are paid to construct a building, in some cases billions when you look at skyscrapers in major cities. So who do you feel more comfortable in choosing to design that building? A computer that is incapable of making a mistake that can cost millions of dollars in over-runs, or an architect who *is* capable of such an error?

But we'll always need **Teachers** right?

In most cases home schooled children do better than public school children. And how well the student does often depends on the teacher. For example, while in high school I had a Latin teacher, and while he was exceptionally knowledgeable, he had absolutely no talent for performing. His voice had no variation in tone.

None.

He droned on like a lawn mower in summer.

I didn't learn a damn thing.

You've likely noticed all the 'Learn on line" video software programs that are specially designed to engage young minds and hold their attention. Products like the Nabi tablet for example.

They are practically a home schooling course in and of itself. The teaching programs created for those devises are tested and retested until they are the absolute pinnacle of knowledge providers.

And regarding online video tutorials, the 'Teachers' aren't the schooled educators presently in our education system, they are professional entertainers who know exactly how to hold the attention of an audience over an extended period of time. Basically they are pitchmen, actors and lead singers for rock bands.

You've likely heard of the extremely popular ***Rosetta Stone*** software for learning foreign languages. Hooked on Phonics? **THERE ARE LITERALLY HUNDREDS OF WEBSITES FEATURING THOUSANDS OF VIDEO TUTORIALS**

THAT HAVE BEEN UPGRADED TO THE POINT WHERE THEY CAN DO A BETTER JOB OF TEACHING ANY SUBJECT BETTER THAN ANY REAL EDUCATOR.

With drugs in school, bullying, and children being shot dead by deranged lunatics, just how long do you think it will take before parents say "enough is enough" pull their children out of school and turn their education over to the software?

Here's another point to consider. Public schools cost money and they don't generate any. They have to be heated and air-conditioned, maintained, insured, have electricity, provide food, have a school nurse all of which comes out of taxpayer money.

But with all the jobs being outsourced or replaced by technology, there won't be enough money to pay for these facilities and so, not only will all public schools close, the responsibility of our future children's education will be in the hands of parents who will likely be working two to three minimum wage jobs just trying to make ends meet.

Doesn't look good does it?

And it gets worse.

You see, I may be lousy at Latin but I'm a whiz at math. And math is the one thing that doesn't lie. True, you can manipulate the statistics, extrapolate questionable research but no matter how you play with the results…

THIS IS WHAT'S GOING TO HAPPEN.

The world is becoming a giant corporation. Soon it won't matter where you were born because all commerce will be international and transacted over the internet. You will live where the work is. Meaning the most valuable employees will live in highly developed countries, like the United States, Canada, Germany, France, Japan, Sweden, Norway, Finland, Denmark, Switzerland, United Kingdom, Italy, Australia and New Zealand and many others as well as up and comers like China, Estonia, Thailand, South Africa, India, Russia, Brazil, and Vietnam.

But, that's for the most valuable employees. The cost of living in those countries will be high, too high for the unskilled or uneducated worker and so, they will have to move to a country where their meager skills are needed.

Poor Third-world countries.

So just imagine. You are born in Los Angeles, California. You grow up with a fine family and friends but you don't do well in school, you don't pay attention, you goof off, don't study, don't learn business...

Don't acquire any needed skills or get the education necessary to get a job in a well-paying profession.

The Los Angeles of the future is a beautiful city, filled with successful professionals, there is no lower income housing, no welfare hotels, and the few service jobs that still exist are filled by people with connections.

The only countries offering jobs to unskilled labor are in dangerous areas with a strong criminal element and unstable government.

And those countries will be the only place you will be able to get a job.

Don't believe that can happen?

Then take a moment to look back on history. When Europe discovered the Americas and saw the Native American's weaponry wasn't as advanced as theirs, they subjugated them and took their land.

When they discovered Africa, they enslaved the indigenous people and sold them all over the world as beasts of burden.

When they came upon the Chinese and Japanese however, there was a different story. They were just as advanced as the Europeans and in some areas even more so.

And so they were left alone

The point is nature preys upon the weak and unprepared. It shows no mercy, and gives no quarter. It rewards the strong and powerful and crushes the needy.

This is why you need to prepare now!

Now here is the nail that will be the greatest job killer in the near future.

It is called the 3D Printer.

Do not make the mistake of thinking this device is some sort of new-fangled machine that prints pictures in 3 dimensions. That is not what it does.

What it does is scan a blueprint of any object, say an adjustable wrench for example, and then CREATES AN EXACT WORKING DUPLICATE!!

This product has more venture capitalists investing in this it than any other. The Motley Fool (one of the most respected investment advisors, don't let the name fool you) claims that it will have a bigger effect on future businesses than the introduction of the computer in the 1980s.

And this is no futuristic prediction. This machine already exists and is being used in many areas of product creation. It is already being used to construct houses (there goes the construction jobs) to make clothing, musical instruments, car parts, furniture, computers, electronic components, artificial limbs and, believe it or not, human organs.

There are numerous videos showing this machine in action on YouTube.

And the most unsettling thing about this machine is that **it can replicate itself!**

So, take a moment and ask, 'Where do you see yourself in five years?' Then factor in the very real possibility that WATSON, the 3D Printer and advanced software are already mainstream in most aspects of business.

Do you know where you NEED to see yourself? You NEED to see yourself making money online.

Even television is beginning to acknowledge the changes in industry. In an episode of the popular sit-com *Modern Family,* the father, a real estate salesman and the mother an executive at a manufacturing company chastise their daughter for not having any interest in returning to college and getting an education. They ask where does she see herself in five years and how does she expect to make a living.

She replies "I have a website where I review the latest fashions, style trends and beauty products. My list of customers, women who want to be kept up to date in the latest trends, is growing every day. Right now it's over 200 hits a day and I've only been at it for six months. They buy the products I feature on my site and with every sale I get a commission. So I think I'll be doing pretty well in five years.

"While your job, Dad, will likely be replaced by videos downloadable to a cell phone of the walk through the house that's for sale and Mom, all you'll be doing all day is watching your computer do your business books and a 3D printer manufacture your product."

She ends with, "Maybe it's *you guys* who should be thinking about *your* future."

On the crime drama *Person of Interest*. One of the main characters purchases a 3D printer to make an exact duplicate of a dead man's hand so he can use it to fool the laser fingerprint scanner and have access to the dead man's vault.

History has shown us that when change begins it moves rapidly. Products and services disappear almost overnight. Their replacements spring up, old products evolve and new ones completely change the way we do business.

And it's happening right now. So let's get you to the front of the line.

How to Get Started

Now that you know the WHY you should start making money online I am now going to show you the HOW.

And because explaining each facet of making money online would require an entire book in and of itself, to save time, on occasion I will refer you to youtube.com video tutorials. They provide well established "How-To" instructions in an easily digestible form.

I believe it's better to SEE how certain procedures are done instead of me trying to explain it in a manner that anyone can understand.

However since I want to reach as many people as possible, I'm going to start at the very beginning to give everyone a chance to succeed.

Note I strongly suggest you read the entire book first before setting out to start making money online.

There are many ways to make money on the internet and you may change your *mind several times on what course you wish to follow as you continue reading. You may decide you want to do all the work yourself or outsource it to experienced professionals. You may decide to change niches or follow an independent path altogether.*

The point is, let what you read here sink in and when you've had the opportunity to consider all your options, then come back and follow your selected path to accrue additional income streams

So… to begin you will need three things.

Step # 1

You will need a computer and internet access.

If you don't have a computer you can likely access one at your local library.

If you have a laptop but no internet access, most coffee shops, food franchises (like McDonalds, Burger King etc.) offer Wi-Fi access as do most bookstores. You've likely seen television shows featuring their characters hanging out at the local Starbucks while working on their laptop or tablet.

Step # 2

Create a business email address.

This address must be different from your personal email. Where your personal email is usually yournamehere@internet provider.com. Your business address should be something that is easy to write and access as you will be using it a lot. Just throw together some line of letters and numbers like Z3r5@serviceprovider.com.

You can create your new business address the same way you created your personal one. If you happen to be VERY new to the internet and don't know how to set up and email account, go to www.google.com

and type YouTube in the search box. You will be taken to YouTube.com

Click on the blue YouTube Official Site heading and you will be taken to the YouTube site.

YouTube features videos on just about every topic imaginable. So if you're brand new to the internet, your two best friends are Google.com & YouTube.com When you combine them there is no limit to what you can learn.

That being said, type these words into the youtube search box *How to set up an email account in gmail.* And watch the video to see how it's done.

Step # 3

Get a notebook to write down website ID's and passwords.

Once you start up-scaling your business you're going to be interacting with others online and downloading specific products and services. And in order to prevent hackers and spammers from filling these sites with garbage and malware, almost all online businesses require you to enter your ID name and password.

So each time you join a website and set up an account **write that ID and password in that notebook**. The notebook is necessary because different sites require different password set-ups. For example one may require at least 7 characters with at least one number, a Capital letter and an underscore. Others only 5 characters and allow no numbers AND some may assign you a password, so you can see why a notebook is essential.

I don't suggest that you put those passwords and IDs in your computer because should your computer fail, you're going to have to do a lot of unnecessary work to catch up and you may be locked out of accounts and services that are essential to your business.

The business email address is so you can acquire information on whatever field you chose to get into. The field you choose is called a _**niche**_. My niche is book publishing. I write and publish books for professionals looking to establish themselves as experts in their industry.

Again that's what I do. _**What you need to decide is what niche you're going to get into.**_

To become successful making money online AND to be able to steadily **INCREASE that income** you will likely need these things.

1) **You will need a product.**
2) **You will need a website**
3) **You will need traffic.**
4) **You will need an auto-responder**
5) **You will need SEO**
6) **You will need backlinks.**

Okay, take a breath. None of that is as hard as it sounds and as promised, I will walk you through it step by step.

So let's start with

How & Where to Get Your Product

I will begin with the most common way to make money on the internet. And that niche is called...

Article Marketing

It's very popular because it doesn't require any money to get started.

Here's how you get a product and sell it.

The process is called affiliate marketing. By joining an affiliate program you can sell products from other companies from their warehouses.

What you do is go to the home page of a big box store, scroll down to the bottom and click on the words that say Affiliates or Affiliate Program. Then sign up (it's Free)

A Link is a word or series of words that when you click on them you are taken to that website

For example: IF you click on this underlined blue Amazon link www.Amazon.com you will be taken to their home page. Once there scroll to the bottom. Among their many services, search for the words Become an Affiliate.

Click on that, which will take you to the affiliate site then follow the instructions on how to become a member. Many of the big stores use affiliate companies. For example Walmart presently uses Linkshare. Target uses ebay affiliate. The process however is the same.

In some cases they will ask you HOW you intent to sell the product you chose. Will you sell it on your blog/website? Through Pay Per Click? Through email marketing? Through Article Marketing? Then they will ask you to choose what products(s) you want to sell and they will create a personalized link for each of those products.

But before you chose, do some research and find out what products are presently popular.

Now this is very important. Make sure you chose a niche that has products that a large number of people are looking to buy

Most large stores offer an affiliate programs, (but not all do)

Just go to their HOME page, scroll to the bottom and click on affiliate or affiliate program. Check the commission ratio to make sure you're getting the best deal.

Then you write a convincing article about a product and at the end of the article include your affiliate link to the product you wrote about.

For example: You just bought a high speed racing bike. It's a great product at a great price that's just starting to get national attention.

Well then, you get the affiliate link for that product from Amazon or Target or whoever is selling it, you write a review telling everyone how great it is, the advantages, the great price and how you personally use it. At the end write something like: If you'd like to know more about this product go to: (add your affiliate link here)

They click on your link, buy the product and because they used *your* link to go the product site, you get a commission.

This is called Bum Marketing and nearly every new affiliate marketer starts out with it

There a countless ways to make money on the internet but nearly every one of them requires some sort of investment. Bum Marketing doesn't. You simply post your articles on sites like www.goarticles.com & www.articlealley.com and others like it.

There is an entire course on all the particulars with many website links so you can reach the most amount of buyers and you could start making money in as little as a week.

For those of you who find this interesting and might want to give it a try go to this link

http://www.bummarketingmethod.com

Sign up using your business email address and start learning and making money.

Keep one thing in mind. This method works but it is WORK INTENSIVE. You will have to write a lot of articles before you start seeing any profit.

The next method is called Blog marketing.

It works similar to article marketing, where you write about a topic on your blog and do a review. (Make sure it is a popular topic with a products you can get affiliates links to)

What you will need to do first is to create a blog/website. There are several ways to do this.

But First Here's What You Need To Know.

Making money on line is not some easy, get rich quick scheme that, by simply pushing a button, you will gain financial windfalls beyond your wildest dreams.

You Will Not!

Although many online marketers will swear that it is and that you can. They all claim that if you do what they do and buy their products, in no time you'll be driving expensive cars and living in tropical paradises.

Again, No You Won't!

You will instead waste months with little to no results and you won't understand why.

Here's why. These people have spent years building their internet business. They have tried numerous businesses most of which failed. BUT, they learned with each failure. Worked incessantly, learned internet marketing from seasoned professionals and slowly discovered methods ***that did work***.

And the reason these people became successful is ***because they discovered what niches and methods worked best for THEM. That doesn't mean that it will work for you!***

Now as I show you proven methods of making money online, understand that the first thing you'll need to learn is ***how to master the basics.***

I can almost guarantee that you will fail if you become dazzled by promises of easy money.

But…

If you carefully learn the basics, and master them step-by-step then you will begin to see progress. It will be slow at first but as you continue to work that progress will increase and money will begin coming in.

EVERY MONTH!

And more importantly, once that money does start coming in you will know exactly what to do with it to further increase your revenue stream.

So here's what you need to do first.

Find a Niche. A Niche is a product or service you wish to sell.

Choose only one niche. Because if you choose more than one you will likely fail. Trust me, that one niche will take up all your time and energy and if you chose a good one it will provide you with a steady income for many years.

Keep in mind not all niches are successful. There are a number of variables. What is your competition? How many people are interested in this niche? Have you chosen a product people are looking to buy?

Plus, there are factors you have no control over. The state of the economy for example. Political correctness. Vindictive creeps who will place bad reviews for your product simply because they ARE creeps.

But! If you do your homework, take the time to select a product or service that people are looking for. If you charge a fair price and over deliver, in time you will likely build a base of satisfied customers who will prefer to buy from you because of your personal service than from some big box store.

However, if you've put a lot of time and effort and the niche you've chosen isn't producing results then drop it and resume your search for the right niche.

Remember, starting an online business is no different than starting a brick and mortar store. A lot of first businesses fail because of inexperience. R.H. Macy has several business flops before hitting it big. Henry Ford filed bankruptcy before creating the Ford Motor Company. And there is always the factor of being at the right place at the right time. Just don't assume you will hit a home run you're first time at bat.

Later, once your mastered online marketing, THEN, you can venture into multiple niches because you'll be able to tell which ones will be successful for you and which ones won't.

By building a strong foundation in internet marketing, by knowing exactly how to present your niche product in a professional manner and in a way that will make viewers want to buy is the most proven way to success.

So, the question is how do you find a niche?

You start out by looking for products or services people want to purchase. This is the most important factor when searching for a niche. You may love a certain topic but if interest is low, **you are creating a hobby not a business.**

Start by going to Amazon and type best-selling products in the search box. Do the same with Wal-Mart, Target and any popular site you can think of. Find out what products are selling. Make a list of the top ten, then go to google and type that product or service into the search box.

Then see *what* companies are selling that product on Google's first page. If the first page is dominated by mega corporations with thousands of backlinks and a high page rankings, you will likely be wasting your time.

Don't expect overnight success with this. You might find a winner with your first try or it may take days or even weeks.

Here's one way to evaluate whether the niche you are considering is on the upswing or one where customers are beginning to lose interest.

Go to Google trends here's the link:

www.google.com/trends

Google Trends is a site where google makes a list of what people are interested in and whether that interest is increasing or decreasing.

So say you're considering all things dollhouses. How to build them, where to buy them, how to decorate them etc.

So before you start investing time and effort, go to Google Trends and type dollhouses in the search box at the top and see if interest in the niche is growing or decreasing (in case you're wondering, it's decreasing at the time of this publication BUT that can quickly change, especially around the holidays.)

It is also important to remember that you will be spending a considerable amount of time and effort featuring this product or service. So it would be wise to choose something you have some interest in.

If for example you find a popular niche with low competition on customized horse saddles but have no interest in horses or saddles, you're likely going into a business you're not going to enjoy.

So choose your niche carefully. Take some time to look around to see what products and services people are selling and pick one that speaks to you.

Another important point is to know whether your niche is popular year round or during a select time.

One fellow online marketer makes a considerable amount of money with his Halloween costume niche, but it only is successful for 6 weeks out of the year. But he fully capitalizes on those 6 weeks and makes a year's worth of profit doing so.

Regarding the dollhouse niche I mentioned earlier, that also is popular mostly during the Christmas and Chanukah season. The rest of the year sales are flat.

You can, however, make the most of those short periods by featuring products in your niche that sell big in short spurts. It's not like you have to pay overhead to keep your online store open. And like I said, a seasonal niche can provide a year's income if done correctly.

So far I've concentrated on showing you how to find and market a **physical** product. However there is CONSIDERABLE money to be made selling software products where the commission can range from 40% to 90% PER SALE

There are many places where you can select a product and market it on your website.

The most popular place is www.clickbank.com Thousands of affiliate marketers go there every day to select products to sell on their sites. Others include www.rapbank.com www.linkshare.com & www.JVzoo.com

The best part is that they are all free to join and you can make a lot of money in commissions once you learn what to look for and how to market it.

Here's how it works. Go to Clickbank.com and sign up for an account (it's Free) then on the above *Clickbank Toolbar* click on **Marketplace** and it will take you to the main page. (*Note* Clickbank has specific criteria regarding the amount and number of sales needed for a payout. Rapbank doesn't)

On the left you will see a line of red boxes. These are the product category niches. There is a considerable number of them ranging from Art & Entertainment, Business & Investment, Home & Garden, Health & Fitness, Computers & Internet, E-commerce & E-Marketing, Self Help and many more.

Peruse the niches (if you haven't already decided on one) and see which ones you feel can be turned into a solid business opportunity.

Now the question is, how do you tell which product offers have the best chance of being successful?

One way to tell is to click on a category that is in your niche. Say you're an experienced carpenter for example, so you select Home & Garden. You scroll through the products until you see one that really interests you and so you click on the header. For example: ***Tom Terrific's super wood-working system***

You're taken to the websites sales page and after looking it over you're convinced this is one of the most amazing products you've ever seen and not only do you want to buy it, you're sure other wood-workers will snap it up as well once they see what it can do.

You are sure this will make you rich!

Well, hold on thar, little buddy. Let's not be hasty. The first thing is you have to find out what your competition is, meaning that once your website starts featuring that product, where on Google is your website going to be placed? On Googles front page? Or page 378?

Another thing to take into account is the sales page itself. Is it professionally done? Does it grab and hold your interest without being gaudy or cheap? Has it convinced you that this product is something you need to have?

Because if it hasn't, how can it convince somebody else and more importantly, how likely is it that you'll make any money with it?

Another important consideration is the whether the product is gaining or losing customers. On way to check that with a Clickbank product is to go to http://cbengine.com

At Clickbank engine you can look up a product and see how it's been selling by scrolling down and clicking on the GRAPH link. If the graph is steadily increasing that's a good sign that the product is worth promoting. If going down however, you might want to keep looking.

Another important factor is to see what the stats for that product is. To see the value, go to the bottom of the offer and check the stats. How much commission will you make on a sale, what's the refund rate and most importantly, what's the **gravity** (GRAV) of the product?

The gravity indicates the number of affiliates presently selling that product to their _lists_ (I'll explain what that is a little later). The higher the gravity, the more successful the product.

Unfortunately, the higher the competition.

However, here's where you can have a distinct advantage if you happen to be experienced in that niche. Because most of the people marketing that product are affiliate marketers not carpenters.

And by starting your sales pitch with something like *"I've made my living as a professional carpenter over the last 20 years and in that time I've never seen a product as valuable as this one for people in the wood-working trade."*

And because of your experience you can spell out the advantages to other carpenters who will quickly see that you know what you're talking about and likely decide to purchase the product.

So you've decided to promote that product so you click on the promote button and then you will type in your ID name and you will be provided with an affiliate link to paste on your website

Here is an example:

http://9e4f0432yvembu12wmqjribl9h.hop.clickbank.net/

This product has been around for a while and is highly recommended on the Warrior Forum. It has a professional video sales page and starts with many, many people touting the success of the product. It is a proven money-maker and an excellent example of a product for those promoting products in this niche.

Here's the link to the reviews

http://www.warriorforum.com/internet-marketing-product-reviews-ratings/127397-reviews-george-browns-google-sniper.html

Now the advantage of promoting a product like this is it has been around for a while and still sells well, it has high gravity rating, a small refund rate and good reviews from those who bought it AND A MONEY BACK GUARANTEE.

On the other hand the refund rate is to be expect since so many people are searching for one click programs that will make them millionaires and that program simply doesn't exist. So they opt for the refund.

However, those who do the work are clearly satisfied, so if your customers are willing to do the minimum amount of work involved, they can make some real money. And far more than they laid out for it.

Remember, there are thousands of ways to make money online and I will show you many throughout this book BUT, if you're serious about becoming a success, **ONLY CHOOSE ONE.**

And when I say chose one **I mean chose One Niche, Not One product.** A niche is the industry and it can be anything. Gaming software, horse saddles, hair care products, weight-loss, rare coins, etc. Or services, like book cover design, website design, copyrighting, financial advice, real estate and so on.

So if you choose hair care products, don't also get involved in horse saddles.

Concentrate on the hair care niche. Feature the whole spectrum of all things hair. Lotions, creams, sprays, conditioners, gels, hair dryers, hair coloring, make up, styles etc. Write reviews on your blog/website and include your affiliate link to those products throughout.

Establish yourself as an expert in the field. Answer questions, invite discussions, get people involved. Contact your affiliate and ask them if you can have a free sample to give away on your site to the one who writes the best review of that product. Conduct surveys, place instructional videos of hair care on your site. Include photos.

The point is there are a million things you can do to promote your site and make money with it. However, if you waffle from one niche to another looking for the big score, you won't have the time necessary to build up your business and that's why most people who start online businesses fail.

The 3 Most Successful Affiliate Products

I am often asked what products sell best online and which ones will make the most money. That's hard to answer because there are a lot a variables in that answer.

Like how much effort is required to make money with that product. How much does the product cost? How much will I have to spend to market it? What is the refund rate? What is the level of customer satisfaction? And so on...

So I went online and found the top three affiliate products in the order of their success.

The first one is, and has been, the top seller for years now and that primarily because it's a very well-run business that provides a very necessary product for those looking to jump to the front of the line when it comes to affiliate marketing success.

1) **The Number One Affiliate Program is: _SBI_**
(Formerly known as Site Build It)

What it does, well to put it frankly, what it does is **everything**!

SBI turns any theme, product, service or store into an online business. And does 90% of the work for you!

First it finds out what type of online venture you want to get into, then it creates keywords, SEO, provides webpage templates then shows you how to build it using only cut and paste tools. It then puts your site online and does a search to attract traffic, then contacts them and presents them with your website. It then gathers email addresses and sends them a newsletter regarding your site and promoting your products. It also provides RSS feeds to potential customers.

Note Their detractors say that should you decide to quit SBI and strike out on your own— which some do once they'll become very skilled—transferring your site and webpages to a different company like WordPress is difficult and time consuming.

I've looked into it and it is no more difficult than moving any site to a different company whether it be Yahoo to WordPress, or Blogger to Wix

If you had a brick and mortar store and had to move your inventory to a different location that would be time consuming too.

In addition I don't suggest you place all your eggs in any one basket. I have websites with Blogger, Yahoo's site builder and WordPress and YES, I have a SBI website.

And out of all of them I like SBI best. And the reason for that is I'm a very busy person. I'm a writer, publisher and marketer so I have little time.

I had a lot of trouble setting up my WordPress site. Then getting the domain name, the webhosting, the THEME, the plug-ins, the widgets and when all was said and done I wasn't even sure the thing was working.

That's not the case with SBI. Through a series of easy to follow videos they walk you through every aspect of setting up an online business and MAKING MONEY WITH IT!

The process is ALL BUSINESS. Everything is labeled, explained, cross- referenced, and split-tested to ensure success.

In addition:

SBI offers a full 90 day money-back guarantee. So there is really no reason why you shouldn't give it a look especially if you're new and want a website that can compete with those that have been professionally created and have been on the web for years.

SBI is a no nonsense professional organization that—through their website tour—makes it very clear why they are the number one affiliate year after year.

Check out their site here:

http://buildit.sitesell.com/publishing101.html

And here's the video tour of what they offer

http://videotour.sitesell.com/publishing101.html

2) The Number 2 Affiliate Program: *Niche Profit Classroom!*

Adam Short, a young, hot-shot is an online marketer who has created over 300 niche websites using his proven formula.

He begins by showing exactly how to make money online, what you will need to do so and why his system works.

He will also provide you with two proven pre-made niche business businesses that you can have up and making you money in as little as a few days.

And he only charges a dollar to get started!

Niche Profit Classroom has a large number of positive reviews and satisfied customers.

Check out his site here:
http://www.nicheprofitclassroom.com/cb/sl/sl_video.html?hop=czar101

3) *The third top Affiliate Program is:*
Marlon Sanders: The King of Step-by-Step Internet Marketing

Marlon is the creator of The Amazing
Formula which has been training
online marketers since its inception
back in 1997.
Updated regularly it is still considered
the best training available to make
money online. It has hundreds of real
testimonials from present day top-tier
online gurus who unashamedly say it
was Marlon's Amazing Formula that
made their original success possible.
You can check it out here:
http://www.marlonsanders.com/secret
s/index2.html

There is one basic theme in each of
these three affiliate programs that I'm
sure is a factor in their continuing
success.

And that is in each case the people
creating these products tell you right
off the bat that online success is
accomplished by hard work, by
offering a highly sought after product
or service and by target marketing the

people who want your product or service.

There is no such thing as push button riches.

Another facet of these three affiliate programs is their unwillingness to waste time or effort with people not willing to do all that is necessary to succeed.

They know their programs work (the fact that they are the top three proves that) that they make affiliates money over the long term.
This is why all offer money back guarantees. SBI gives you 90 days to decide if their product works for you. Marlon offers ***Triple Your Money Back*** if The Amazing Formula doesn't work for you within a YEAR and Adam is so sure of his program, he only charges a dollar to get started.

My point here is that anyone, with the right knowledge, the willingness to learn and the perseverance to keep at it until the money starts pouring in will very likely succeed. (Please note that legally I cannot guarantee that you will make money with any online program. And that's because I do not know you personally, or your work habits.)

What to Watch Out For

Among the many ways to make money online is something called MLM. That stands for multi-level marketing.
I will point out that there is nothing illegal about it and in many cases joining one will provide you will a solid education on how to make money online.

The only problem is it's likely those providing you with that information

will be the only ones making money out of that deal.
Not you.

Here's how it works.
They offer you a free membership in their money making venture. It usually has thousands of members who enthusiastically praise the organization and its leaders.
So after a while you start thinking this is something you probably should get in on.
So you join their beginner program for a nominal fee of somewhere around $20.00 a month.

And with that program you receive a number of video tutorials on marketing their product online, and once you convince someone else to join the $20 a month membership through your link, you get to keep that $20.00 and apply it to your own monthly membership, which means your own membership is now FREE!

AND... the more people you convince to join, the more money you make. Just note that you don't make all of it however. Usually the money made from every third or so sale goes to the person who got you to join. But the good thing about it is that every third sale of your ***downline*** (those are the people who signed up with your link) goes to you. So hypothetically, the more members you and your downline sign up, the more money you get.

And on top of that, the company offers ELITE training. Special super-duper training that only the top money makers know. And these ELITE training packages aren't cheap. They go from a few hundred dollars each to a few thousand dollars, with ABSOLUTELY no guarantee that you will make any money.
Nor do they offer refunds.

Another way they use to sell you on their MLM program is to have giant conferences every three months or so that you can attend (for a price) and hob-nob with the "Big Money Online People" who will likely share some of their "Making Big Money Online" tips with you.

Even better during the festivities they roll out the "Giant Checks with the Giant Commissions" and have a special ceremony to award those who did well and made a lot of money.

These people are almost ALWAYS those who have spent A Lot of money to learn how to make that money.

The thing is, you can learn the same techniques for free by watching YouTube videos on MLM marketing.

The point is when all is said and done, you might find yourself out of a lot of money and have nothing to show for it.

BUT in all fairness, there are some who have a real knack for this kind of selling and do well right out of the gate.

In that case my recommendation would be to first find out how well you do with selling the $20 program. Because if you don't do well with the simple stuff, odds are, regardless of the advanced training, you're not going to make any real money selling the more complex stuff.

However, some people make a lot of money! A LOT OF MONEY.

And in almost every case they are the people who have been in online marketing for years and know every facet of the industry.

Do you? Or are you, like most of those roped into MLM still struggling to make your first sale?

Personally I suggest you steer clear of these organizations. There are many, many better ways to make money online. And more reputable ways to earn a living

Now let's move onto

Creating your Business Website/Blog

So let's say you've chosen your niche and are ready to create a website/blog.

The difference between a website and a blog is that…

There is No Difference.

When you create a website on Word Press you will have the choice to make it a static page or a non-static page.

A static page is like a store front. It features the stores products, prices, pictures, perhaps some reviews, special offers, coupons etc.

An example would be the big box stores websites.

A non-static page is a website that changes regularly, features articles on topics that either interest the website owner, or as a marketing vehicle for the niche products the author is promoting. It has sidebar links to affiliate products (like AdSense) and builds a following by including an opt-in page for a newsletter so they can advise his or her followers on the latest updates regarding their niche.

If you're completely new to this, here are instructions for the…

<u>Beginner:</u>

Since you are new, I want to make it possible for you to set up your blog/website with the least amount of trouble or effort.

So go to http://blogger.com sign up and follow the simple instructions on setting up your blog/website. It's free and convenient and it gives you access to Google's AdSense program which provides the option to feature products on your sidebar, which if people click on those links and buy, you get a commission. Here's the link:

www.adsense.com

Now here is an important thing to remember. Using a free site is good when you're just getting started and want to get your feet wet to see if making money online is something you want to pursue.

BUT…

A free site is not the place to set up a serious business.

Since it is a free site, that means someone else owns it. Which is why your website, instead of being johndoe.com it is johndoe.**blogspot**.com

In Bloggers case it is owned by Google. This means they can, and without notice or reason, shut down your site. Which means all the work you put into it and all the products you feature are erased.

There are a number of horror stories of affiliate marketers losing their blogger sites which had thousands of loyal followers with no explanation or reason given.

But it stands to reason these sites were shut down because Google HATES SEO.

They want all sites to be ranked on their age content and natural backlinks etc. Unfortunately, you need to already be a Fortune 500 company to come into all those things naturally so that's why we need SEO to level out the playing field.

Which is why Google is regularly rolling out new and more effective ways to shut down search engine optimization (Panda & Penguin Programs) so if you're serious about making money online the sooner you get a WordPress account the better.

So my advice? If you're new to this by all means start with a blogger account. I've had one for over 5 years http://zackaryrichards.blogspot.com which has had over 25,000 visitors primarily due to my blog posts. However, *I make the majority of my online money selling on my Word Press sites*.

For the Intermediate Online Marketer:

This is the level most affiliate marketers are at, and the point where they've learned enough about online business to create a permanent website, have chosen a niche and are ready to start a full time business.

Which means you're ready to create a WordPress website.

And it also means you're ready to invest a little money. To begin, you will need to purchase a domain name. For example Willieswidget.com or sallysdollhouse.com

By purchasing a domain name you have taken the first step in establishing yourself as a serious business. Also notice that there is no (dot.)blogspot or (dot.)freebie following your businesses name.

Whenever possible choose a .com domain name i.e.: tastypickles**.com**

A .net is all right but people automatically assume all sites are .com sites and you don't want your potential customers going to tastypickles**.com** when your site is tastypickles**.net**

When choosing your business name, choose one that contains words a lot people search for on Google, yet has very little competition.

This is one of the most important factors in becoming a success online so make a note of this. The goal of every online business is to be featured on the first page of a Google search. Preferably in the top spot or as close as possible to it.

63

Millions search on Google every day from everywhere, so being on the first page of a popular keyword is your ticket to online success.

Now lets' discuss what a keyword is. *A keyword is the word (or words) a person types into the Google search box. Or Yahoo or Bing etc.*

For example. Say I want to lose weight, so I go to Google, type **weight loss** in the search box and am instantly taken to Google's first page for that topic.

The first ten or so websites featured will likely have the words **weight loss** somewhere in the name of their site. For example: Quickweightloss.com or tenminuteweightloss.com or instantweightloss.com so I click on those sites, and if I like what they offer I buy their product.

Now here is where many looking to make money online go off the rails and wind up spinning their wheels.

You wouldn't open a Mom & Pop store next to a Wal-Mart so don't create a website that will be in competition with mega-sites like webmd.com dr.oz.com menshealth.com weightwatchers.com etc.

Frankly if you created a site called billsweightloss.com your site will likely be buried on page two-thousand of that Google search.

So when creating your site and selecting your niche always remember that the keyword(s) with the MOST searches and the LEAST competition is the surest path to online success.

And don't limit yourself to common themes like weight loss, health & fitness, dog training, relationships and making money. The competition for those niches is HUGE and you don't need that starting out.

And remember it doesn't have to be a thing you're selling. It could also be a service.

For example when a friend of mine was downsized from his editing and copywriting position for a major publisher, he decided to start his own online business.

So he created a website on WordPress and then went to www.fiverr.com

Fiverr.com is a website where you can purchase a vast number of services for a mere five dollars. For example: Some do website graphics. Logo design, background music, copyrighting, business, SEO, and a number of other needed services for only five dollars.

So my friend signed up and offered professional editing services for one dollar a page for the first five pages

Now keep in mind that he was well aware that he would have to do a lot of work for very little money BUT his goal was to establish his editing business.

Because he is a very talented editor, he quickly established himself as the 'go-to' guy when professional editing was needed.

Novelists began visiting his website to get free quotes for a professional edit of their books. In less than a year his online editing business was making him more money than he made working for the publishing company.

And he doesn't have to commute or wake up at some ungodly hour or play office politics. He simply is able to do what he loves and gets paid for doing it.

BUT! He was also smart enough to learn online marketing and get the information he needed to get his website listed on Google's first page.

So take a moment and consider selling a service online. There is also the option of selling a video tutorial online.

What I mean by this is that there are hundreds of people creating instructional videos of them showing others their particular area of expertise.

So for example. Mary is a top notch-quilter. Has won several trophies and sells her wares at various craft shows.

To make additional income Mary could make a step-by-step video course showing exactly how she create these stunning quilts and sell those videos online at a site that specializes in marketing step-by-step videos.

In fact there are a step-by-step video courses that teaches you exactly how to make a step-by-step video course of your own.

However, if you are already comfortable before the camera then just create a video using the video software that came with your computer. For example Movie maker for a PC and Quicktime for a Mac.

Both are fine for whipping up a quick promotional video.

If you want to create a more professional video then go to the next step and purchase a commercial program. The one I use is NCH Video Pad http://www.nchsoftware.com/videopad/index.html?ref=4068062

The easy to use software comes with a video tutorial that walks you through each aspect of video creation. It also comes with a 30 day free trial, so you get to see if you like it before buying.

Another way to promote your product is with a voice over.

When creating your blog post, feature a picture of the product you're promoting and connect it to a voice over

For example: "Hello and welcome to Bob's Wood-Working Shop. Today I have something I think you're really going to like. It's the MSK4000 miter saw with attachable...blah, blah blah etc.

Doing a voice over gives more of a personal touch and most people won't bounce out of your site while you're still talking, and that's a definite advantage.

For this I use NCH Wavepad
http://www.nch.com.au/wavepad/index.html?ref=4068062

Again easy to use with video tutorial and free trail.

So back to finding the right keyword(s) title for your site. One that has a lot of searches but very little competition.

Back in the good old days there was a site called Google Keyword Tool. It was the online marketers' bible and the best place to find perfect keywords for your niches.

Unfortunately Google considered that rigging the game and so they replaced google keyword tool with Google Keyword Planner.

It's nowhere as good.

So how do you find the right keywords for your niche? Here are your options, purchase a keyword finder or go on fiverr and pay to have someone with a high customer satisfaction rating to find the best keywords for your niche.

Affiliate marketer Pat Flynn has several excellent tutorials on keyword research so I suggest you check out his videos on YouTube.

The keyword(s) will be part of the name of your business so if possible chose one as short as possible and one that's easy to remember. For example

www.dollhousesRus.com or
www.bestsourmashmix.com

One last thing to remember. This is a business blog so focus on content that reflects your niche. It is not a place to give your political, religious or social views. The goal is to present INTERESTING information about your niche and why subscribing to your newsletter, buying your products and regularly visiting your site is something they should do.

Now let's move on to step # 2

So here's where we stand. You have found a niche that has a large number of buyers and have discovered a keyword in that niche that has a high number of searches but very little competition.

You're on your way. So the next thing you need to do is purchase a domain name. By doing so you are establishing your first real online business. Buying a domain name isn't expensive, usually under $12.00 a year.

There are many places where you can purchase a domain name. But first you have to find out if the name you have chosen is available. So to find out go to Namecheap here's the link https://www.namecheap.com/?utm_source=none&utm_medium=Affiliate&utm_campaign=52164

Type in the name you've chosen and see if you can buy it.

If you've chosen a name that has a high number of searches and little competition it will likely be available. If not and you really want that domain name go to the website and see if it is active. If not, the owner may be willing to sell the domain name for as little as $20.00. But I'd be suspicious because if the name was really good, why is the site not being used?

But let's say the domain is available and you buy it. The next step is to get a web-hosting account to place that website on the internet.

Before you do either, here's a point to consider. Most domain name sellers offer web-hosting and most web-hosters also offer domain name sales.

It is recommended that you **DON'T** purchase both services from the same company. The reason for this is if one of those companies runs into legal or financial trouble and gets shut down, *you won't lose your business* because your domain name company and web hosting company are separate. If they are the same then you may lose access to your account until that company's problems are straightened out.

For example I purchase my domain names from www.namecheap.com and my webhosting from www.hostgator.com

Both companies have excellent reputations and have never had problems BUT why take chances?

Pay close attention now because a mistake here can cause a lot of problems down the road.

In order to work, your domain name provider and your web host need to be linked together.

When you purchase a webhosting plan from www.hostgator.com they will send you an email. And in that email is a DNS code that you need to cut & paste in your domain name provider. <u>It can take up to 72 hours for that domain name to become active on the net</u> AND additional time before your new site is discovered by search engines. Also note that the Free Easy Landing Page site http://getelpp.com has EXACT video instructions on how this is done. If you are unsure of your present skills then I suggest you go there and have a look to make sure you've got it right.

And once you have established a website with your chosen niche or service just imagine how well that will work out for you during the holiday season, when tens of millions are on the net searching for Christmas presents and keep in mind they aren't buying just one product, they are buying *MANY* products.

And there is no limit to the number of internet websites you can create and get running.

For example: Say you create a website called Bestdeckfurniture.com. At that site you have 25-30 links featuring the best (and costly) deck & patio furniture and a large number of high performing keywords.

On another website you feature custom car accessories called bestcaraccessories.com Again you have 25-30 affiliate links set up and running 24/7 with high performing keywords

On another you have baby car seats. The site is called safestbabycarseats.com Again 25-30 links running 24/7 with great keywords

Now imagine the income you could have by simply creating 25-30 SITES like those mentioned above.

And here is where the magic comes in.

Once the websites are created, you don't have to do anything else. Just sit back and watch the money roll in.

Now granted creating 25-30 specialty sites is a lot of work, is very time consuming and flat out exhausting.

So what do you do?

You do what all the major corporations are doing. You OUTSOURCE!

"Wait!" you say. *"Won't outsourcing be expensive and won't it be difficult to find a qualified individual?"*

Not at all!

Which brings us back to our old friend fiverr.com

On Fiverr you can find someone who will do the work for you, and is ranked by customer satisfaction. So for just five dollars you can get just about any service you need, from web design, to graphics, to SEO to anything your specific niche requires.

So keep that in mind when you set up your website and want something that looks professional and welcoming to potential buyers.

Although creating a blogger website was easy and not all difficult. Setting up a Word Press website requires some knowledge.

Because WordPress updates its site regularly, any instructional video link on how to set up your WordPress website I would provide will probably be outdated by the time this book is published.

Therefore I suggest you go to Youtube or Google search boxes and type in *How to set up a WordPress website* and click on the post or video that is the most recent. You also might want to give a look at http://marketingeasystreet.com as Brian G. Johnson often provides updated info on setting up WordPress sites.

Another option is to outsource it to fiverr.com and have all the work done for you. It will probably cost a little more than the usual five dollars if you want all the bells and whistles but you can likely get it all done for under $20.

And now for the most important question:

HOW DO I GET PAID?

In many instances, product providers like Amazon and Clickbank do direct deposit to your checking account. Most however prefer to do all transactions on PayPal.

PayPal is a highly respected world-wide organization that pays and receives money for you. This way you won't have to keep using your credit card when you want to buy a product or service, PLUS won't have to keep giving out your checking account number every time you make a sale.

There are several ways to load money into and out of your PayPal account. Please note that this can take several days if done through standard banking channels.

A faster way to do it is to pick up a MoneyPak card from any Big Box Store or supermarket and load the money directly onto it.

PayPal works through MoneyPak so any making or receiving of payment can be done instantly through that method. I usually keep $100 in my PayPal account and transfer anything over that to my checking account.

I like using PayPal because that, although I've never had a problem giving my credit and/or debit card information online, I prefer that my PayPal account handle it so I don't have to keep sending my personal checking account info over the Internet.

Now it's time to take the next step.

How to Drive Traffic to Your Website

Traffic is the internet term for customers.

And without traffic you don't have a business.

Here's a mistake many new comers to making money online make. They take the time to find a good niche, find excellent products to market, get a domain name, get a web-hosting account, set up the site themselves or have it done for them (fiverr. com for example) have top notch graphics, great content...

And get no sales.

Why? Because there are over 4 million websites online and nobody knows who you are, what you're selling or that you even exist. SO...the first thing you need to do is get your website known!

How do you do this?

After your website is set up and online go to

https://support.google.com/webmasters/answer/35769?hl=en

This is googles webmaster site. Register your site with them and follow their instructions and you'll be recognized by search engines in a short period of time. Otherwise it could take weeks and sometimes months before you can be found on a search engine search.

How else do you get your website known?

You do it the same way all businesses do. You advertise, you network, you go on forums, and most importantly you set up a squeeze (opt-in) page

A simple no frills opt-in page can be created on any auto-responder but it often helps to have an eye catching template to entice the viewer and to hopefully get them to fill in their name and email address and become a subscriber.

The FREE site I use is Easy Landing Page Pro http://getelpp.com

The real advantage of using this site is that there is an instructional video at the top left of each step. So if you're new to opt-in (squeeze pages) the videos will skillfully walk you through the process so you can take advantage of each and every traffic generating opportunity.

Basically it's a fill-in-the-blanks set up.

At this point however you will need to have a WordPress site with domain name and hosting already in place, because you will need a place for the opt-in page to redirect your subscriber once they sign up.

Once you have completed the process, sign up with your business email to make sure the link is working

NOTE In order to keep the names of your subscribers you will have to be registered with an auto-responder. And that process will be explained in the following chapter

Next you go on Facebook!

Another way to get traffic is set up a Facebook (fan) or business page. Mine is www.facebook.com/aripublishing

Then, go to the top left *Search for people places & things* and type in your niche. For example, make money online, woodworking, fishing lures, sporting equipment etc.

It will then provide you with a list of people and organizations presently involved in that niche.

For example: As a writer and publisher I typed in Writers Groups and discovered numerous Facebook writers & publishers groups that I was able to present my products to and interact with.

Promotion in Social Media:

As mentioned in the beginning of this book the Internet is becoming the driving force of business and a world onto itself. I've met more people on the net than I've met in real life and I certainly do more business on the net than I do through the usual channels of book fairs and conferences.

And if you're looking for customers then the place to go is FACEBOOK!

If you're not on Facebook then you're missing out on selling your product to over ONE BILLION subscribers

That's right Facebook has over One Billion subscribers and you have access to them all.

So how do you get access to all these people?

You Open A Facebook Store!

You may not be aware of this but Facebook is a wonderful place to conduct business. You can directly contact people who are interested in what you have to sell. You can make up ads and have them seen by hundreds of thousands of people! You can join Facebook groups and forums and be able to talk directly to people who have the same interests as you AND may be able to give you tips on building your business and customer base. So if you haven't joined

Facebook do so now. And here is how you start:

First create a personal page. Just go to Facebook.com and follow the simple instructions. This is necessary because you cannot create a business page without a personal page. Then once you have your personal page up and running, search for people you know and ask them to "FRIEND" you

Then create a business page (otherwise known as a fan page) and this is easily done. Now that you have a personal page all you need do is get on Facebook and on the top right inside the blue bar your will see a gear shaped icon. Click on that and scroll down to Create Page.

Click on that then chose from the six boxes what product or service you intend to market. Then click on the category (niche) name your product then click the box saying you will follow Facebook's terms and conditions. You should give them a look. Even though it's pretty standard, they have certain rules regarding how and where you can display your product and what products you cannot sell or display.

Another way to get yourself 'Out There" is to purchase a few traffic building programs.

BUT before you lay out any money, make sure the software or PDF has excellent reviews, is being sold through an accredited company (Clickbank, Linkshare, Rapbank, commission junction, JVZoo, etc.) **and that it comes with a money-back guarantee.** Also **DO NOT** pay for expensive programs that promise unlimited traffic. Not because they don't exist, but because those expensive programs generally are set up outside regular providers like Clickbank and are run through their own company so they don't have to pay commissions to the providers.

There are many that, for a few thousand dollars, CAN make you a lot of money. Far more than the cost of buying that product. But they use complex methods and procedures you won't likely understand until you've been at this for a while. So don't be swayed by that *"You need to <u>go all in</u> to become a success"* nonsense the marketing gurus propose.

Another reason why you shouldn't move too quickly is that you can't tell the frauds from the legit businesses yet. And they are out there!

Are you aware that the frauds have literally thousands of members and have gotten them by using the best sales page creators in the business? These sales page masters get upwards of $50,000 for each page they create. They're paid that kind of money because those pages generate millions in revenue!

<u>Here's another trick:</u>

You go to a sales page and see dozens of positive testimonials for that product. Person after person gushing about how good the product is.

Did you know you can buy testimonials online?

So until you are able to spot the frauds, stay away from any product that isn't guaranteed by a recognized provider. Start small, buy inexpensive traffic tutorials from the Warrior Forum (Warrior Plus) after reading the reviews to make sure it's worth the investment. Then some from Clickbank and the others. A lot of it is very informative and helpful and WILL make you money, however some of it is crap.

But with a recognized provider you can easily get your money back. I've done it on a couple of occasions. Just make sure you want what you're buying. Customers who request too many refunds, sometimes get barred from the provider's website.

Just so you know.

As for getting traffic, there are many ways to do it. We'll go over some of the easiest methods first.

The best traffic is paid traffic. Why? Because they are proven buyers and you can purchase as much or as little traffic as you want.

There are a large number of places where you can buy traffic. Hop on Google and search for paid traffic for whatever niche you've chosen. But remember! Only buy traffic from places that feature buyers in your niche. If you are selling rare coins, don't buy traffic from a site that features traffic for dog training.

One of the most popular sites is

www.safe-swaps.com

Then there are what is called solo ads.

Here's how it works.

Research ezines in your niche, (with the example of rare coins you would go to google and type in rare coin ezines in the search box) have a look at the sites then in the *'contact us'* section email them and ask if they would sell you ad space on their e-zine. But before you buy, find out what their open rate is. Meaning how many of their subscribers actually open the emails and read them. Because an ezine can have 10,000 subscribers but if only 25 or say actually open and read them, you are likely wasting money.

Of course you should also shop around to get the best price for the most 'eyeballs'.

A more complex and costly way to get traffic is to use data brokers.

Data brokers collect information on peoples interests, like magazine subscriptions, niche purchases, website members etc. They have THOUSANDS of email addresses that you can purchase and present your offer to.

Note I do not recommend this method to those of you new to making money online. It's expensive to run and requires a good deal of knowledge to choose the lists that will convert into sales.

There is one advantage however and that is these data brokers often offer free samples of several hundred (sometimes thousands) of email listings that you can use for free to see how well they convert. If you do find a good one that does well for your product niche, it might be a worthwhile investment.

Again I suggest you get a firm handle on your overall skills first before trying this method but, if you already know your way around then here are a few of them to check out.

Lists.nextmark.com

Marigoldtechtech.com

The other type is organic traffic.

This is what you get when people find your site through a Google search. Generally it because they were interested in something you blogged about, found your site interesting and signed up for your newsletter

Organic traffic, when you get it, is the best traffic for the long term.

Say your niche is rare coins. Several times a week, write a blog post on your site with interesting facts about coins you've acquired and the advantages of buying from you. The more posts you write with informative content the more the search engines will recognize you and move you up the Google ladder.

And here is a good way to accomplish that. There is a software product that searches the web for forums, blogs and Facebook pages pertaining to your site's niche. It then connects you to them which gives you the opportunity to advise them of your product or service & leave your URL which also establishes a backlink to your site. I have it and it's pretty amazing. Have a look here.

Buzzbundle.com

Then create a newsletter, send it out a couple of times a month and offer a free product in your niche to anyone who signs up.

For example: On my online education site http://theundergroundcollege.com I give away FREE e-books on a variety of topics. If my subscribers are interested in the topic they download it (they are in PDF form so you don't need a Kindle) and if not interested they simply delete the email.

Now here is where your actual business begins, so pay close attention. If there is one saying you will likely hear hundreds of times while making money online it's…

THE MONEY IS IN THE LIST!

This is why it is extremely important that you collect email addresses so you can advise your subscribers of any and all upgrades to the products you offer.

"Yeah, but I don't want to come off as pushy and salesy," you say.

Understood, but ask yourself this question. Are you annoyed when you learn there is a new version of a product you love?

Do you get irritated when the new cars are rolled out each September? Get ticked when Apple or Samsung roll out their latest cell phones? Shake your head in disgust when Black & Decker present their latest wood-working product?

Of course not! Why would you? You love this stuff and are very interested in the latest versions and advances in technology.

As a writer and a publisher I am always interested in the latest trends in writing and publishing. In fact, I NEED to know what they are in order to continue to compete in the field.

And that's exactly why you won't come off as "salesy". You are providing your customers with the information they want.

So, how do you get this "List"?

The Next Step is:

How & Why You Need to Get an Auto-Responder

An auto responder collects names and emails addresses for you so you can contact your subscribers when you come upon a product you think they would be interested in.

This product however is only necessary once you begin getting regular traffic. Otherwise you can simply ask those who visit your site to email you at your business email address if they'd like further information.

An auto responder becomes necessary when your site become popular and is visited regularly. If you attempt to send an email to more than 10 people most email providers won't send because it will be viewed as spam. And it can become a real pain to have to keep sending out 9 emails at a time and even then you might be shut down because of the AMOUNT of emails you are sending.

That's when it's time to get an auto responder.

For example, I recently came across a software product that takes a Microsoft WORD document and automatically converts and uploads it to Kindle, perfectly formatted each and every time.

If you know anything about uploading to Kindle you realize what a godsend this software is.

And so I made my subscribers aware and created a link on my www.zackaryrichards.blogspot.com website.

How did I do this? Well I have an account with aweber.com and with their software I created what's called an opt-in box on the right side of all my websites.

What it does is collect the names and email addresses of everyone who wants to be informed of new products and upgrades in that particular niche.

It's not spam. It's not something hackers use to corrupt your website. It is instead a highly sophisticated software programs that permits people with similar interests and hobbies to be kept in the loop when something new and exciting comes on the market.

How it works is simple. You email the people who opt-in to your site every so often when a new product or software that is related to your niche is rolled out.

When received, they can purchase the product, become an affiliate themselves or if they have lost interest in the niche, opt-out by clicking on the **unsubscribe** link at the bottom of every email.

And once they've opted-out, they are off your list.

This is what you need to know:

__Creating a list of subscribers is the most important aspect of your business because without a list you don't have customers and if you don't have customers, you can't make money online.__

What you have is a hobby, and a very time consuming one, I might add.

So, once you've decided that making money online is what you want to do, give up the free site, purchase a domain name, get a web hosting account, create a word press site and get an auto-responder.

Chose whatever website provider that bests suits you. I use both www.wordpress.org and SBI for my businesses.

As for auto-responders the two most popular are Aweber.com and getresponse.com Give both a look and decide which one better suits your individual needs.

As for the webhosting, here's the link I use: Hostgator It cost only a dollar for the first month so give it some thought once you start collecting followers

Just do those few things, my friends, and for under $50 you can have your own legitimate online business.

Then to further advance your business and establish yourself as an authority in your chosen niche, after a year or so of regular blogging, collect all the blog posts and have it turned into a published book

> *Note* stop by www.aripublishing.com when you're ready to have that book made. It's their specialty.

The same method goes for any product from customized bowling balls to video game guides to whatever.

One internet marketing friend told me it doesn't matter what you're selling. From the most expensive product to a dime a dozen knick-knack, it all comes down to finding people who want to buy it.

So, keep that in mind. Too often we fall so in love with our product that we fail to see why it isn't selling.

If it isn't selling there are only two reasons.

> *1) The people who want it don't know about it*

2) *You have not made it interesting enough for them to want it.*

In either case you have to take action.

In my novel, How to Write, Publish & Market your Novel into a Bestseller, I remind indie authors that if they choose an obscure title like The Halmlind Way for a book that shows how to increase your intelligence, a Google search will only come up with 4 results. However, if you change the title to *Increase Your Intelligence the Halmlind Way* the results jump to 81,000 when people type in the keyword, *increase your intelligence.*

My point? If your product isn't selling you need to find out why.

Which brings us to our Next Step.

SEO: Which Stands for Search Engine Optimization.

Here's how it works. When someone types in a search on Goggle (or Bing or Yahoo) the search engines start looking for sites that contain those keyword(s) and compiles them according to content, age, Page Rank, backlinks and other factors.

The better optimized your site, the better position you will be in when people search your keywords. There are a number of SEO gurus who have mastered the art of getting ranked on Google's first pages. The one I follow is Alex Becker's www.source-wave.com It is a FREE newbie to master course on Search Engine Optimization and something you should seriously consider watching and learning from.

It's basic logic. In order to make money online, you need customers. The best way to get customers (traffic) is to have your website on Google's first page. And the best way to get on Google's front page is for your site to be optimized for search engines. Ergo you need SEO.

In fact, one of the most successful niches is SEO itself

TRAFFIC THROUGH SEO

Here's a hypothetical example:

As your rare coin niche begins making money you realize that you've become very good at SEO (search engine optimization) and people are asking you to optimize their sites for them.

And so is born a new niche for you, SEO.

You start by charging a fee to optimize sites and for getting them on Googles first page.

An example of taking your business to the next step is Brian Moran of Get 10k fans. He started with a baseball site and a fan page on Facebook and, like most new internet marketers, he was having a tough time.

Then he began to notice that his Facebook site was getting traffic. So he began experimenting and discovered that he not only was he able to get subscribers, he was able to convert them into BUYERS.

What's more, he discovered getting Facebook traffic was his real talent and so he created his get 10k fans website on Facebook which has since grown to over 350,000 subscribers.

Any successful business person will tell you that the original business they started out to create is considerably different than the business they became successful with.

I can tell you from personal experience that when I start writing a book I always have a pretty good idea of what will happen.

Except it never turns out that way.

What I wind up creating is a hybrid.

Take the time to learn to sell online so when opportunities arise **THAT ARE ALREADY PROVING THEMSELVES TO BE MONEYMAKERS ON YOUR NICHE you can start monetizing them!**

Let's go back to our guy who discovered that his SEO skills were making him better money than his regular rare coin website.

Then he gets a brainstorm and realizes that he could use his SEO skills to create first page professional sites for various disciplines (dentistry, real estate, accounting, investing, plastic surgery etc.)

So he creates a few then contacts people working in those professions and asks how much would it be worth to them to have their business featured on Google's first page. Then he reminds them that Google's first page gets several million hits a day, so it would increase their customer base considerably.

He then points out that the business world is going digital and that those who hesitate WILL BE LEFT BEHIND.

Remember the old saying, when starting a business the three most important factors are:

1) Location
2) Location

3) Location.

And there is no better location than being the first page of Google for your niche.

So he begins a new niche of being a type of internet landlord. One where he gets paid a good amount of money each month by renting out his site to professionals who want to be featured on Googles first page for their discipline.

Another good way to get solid SEO, traffic and Backlinks is to buy a website at website auctions

Sites like RegisterCompass.com or Expireddomains.net or Flippa.com or GoDaddy domain auctions just to name a few, routinely offer websites for sale that the owners have abandoned or have just forgotten about.

And this happens far more often than you realized. For example: A website for actress Olivia Wilde was put up for auction and a very astute marketer snapped it up for under $100.

I assume the original owner of that website didn't realize what he was losing. Olivia Wilde is one of the most beautiful women in the world and her name is searched on Google THOUSANDS of times a day. It had a great PR rating, backlinks and SEO

After taking ownership of the site the new owner monetized it with affiliate products relating to health, beauty and fashion and is making a killing with it being on Google's first page!

Do you have any idea what that website can sell for now!?

Think about this. What if you created a website for an up and coming celebrity? We'll use a fictitious name like John Famous.

So you see the possibilities of his career going viral so you go to namecheap.com and see if the domain name www.johnfamous.com is available.

You discover that it is AND www.johnfamous.net is available as well. So you purchase them both, monetize the hell out of them, optimize the site and lock in a ton of high quality back links by going to places like www.backlinkmetro.com

By the time John Famous has his first hit, he is making you $300 a day, after that you're making up to $3000 a day. But the rock & fashion industry is unstable so you sell the two websites for a few hundred grand!

Billionaire Donald Trump says he became a billionaire when he realized that all he had to do to create a successful business was to take undervalued property, fix it up and sell it.

That process works the exact same way for underutilized and abandoned websites.

You simply need to put in the time and effort to find them.

And don't kid yourself into thinking it's all no risk. Because John Famous just might say something incredibly stupid and find himself a person non-grata in the media. Don't believe me?

Ask Mel Gibson and Michael Richards.

Traffic by PPC:

Here's how it works. You select a product on Clickbank (or similar site like Linkshare or Commission Junction) and create a squeeze page, otherwise known as an opt-in page. To create one you will need two things:

An auto responder and a squeeze page to cut and paste your auto responder code on. There are two main auto responders (and several less known) they are aweber.com and get response.com and you can download a free squeeze page set up from easy landing page here's the link: http://getelpp.com

Backlinks:

Backlinks are websites that you link to and are linked to you. The more high quality backlinks you obtain the better you site will rank and the higher your site will be on Google pages.

The Next Step is

Backlinks and Why They're Necessary to Your Online Money Making Venture

Backlinks are attachments that 'link' one site to another. For example I have three websites all linked to one another.

When I want to place a link on a respected site with a strong PR rating I simply write a supportive comment in the comment section and type in my URL for example

I've read your post and thought it quite informative. Thanks!

http://theundergroundcollege.com

Do about ten a day.

The best backlinks to get are .gov and .edu links because they are the most respected and authoritative. So if you are linked to them, and they are linked to you, the search engines will group you in with these respected and authoritative sites and your ranking will improve.

Another way to get backlinks is to swap links. A *You link to my site and I'll link to yours.* This is completely legit and a good way to hook up with people in your niche. There is a site that offers this service and it's called www.link2me.com

You sign up, submit your site link for review and if it passes their requirements they will provide you with 5 free links a day. Which is a good and steady way to build your sites Page Rank and push it up Google's searches.

You can also buy links from places like www.backlinkmetro and www.blackhatlinks.com

Just remember Google frowns on purchasing links so make sure that if you're going to buy links they are high quality and are not dumped on your site all at once. That is a definite red flag so talk to your supplier and see if they can 'drip' the links to your website. And remember it's better to get smaller amount of top quality links than it is to get thousands of low quality ones.

The Last Step:

Putting it All Together to Make Money Online

It will take a while to get a firm grip on how to make money online but if you follow the tips and suggestions I've outlined in this book you'll be off to a good start.

Remember don't go chasing after windmills. Choose your niche and work at making money with it. Purchase courses and tutorials on making money with your niche from respected and highly recommended professionals who offer their services through accredited marketplaces.

Be VERY wary of marketers who offer products through their own sites. Yes they will have banners and official looking stickers offering 30-60 day money back guarantees and full product support but, I have run into a couple of sites that don't supply the product once you've paid for it and any support ticket you file with their website for a refund will be ignored.

And be especially wary of those sites that claim to have a software product that does something absolutely phenomenal. Something that will sky-rocket your sales and put you on the Googles front page.

Frankly if it's not being offered on well-known marketplaces like Clickbank, Commission Junction, Rapbank, Warrior Forum, JVZoo, Linkshare, etc. I wouldn't risk it until you become familiar with the site and the people running it. Once you are sure they aren't some "here today, gone tomorrow" outfit, and have seen a number of positive reviews on WarriorPlus, then go-ahead.

I would like to point out that my experience with making money online has shown me that **The VAST majority of Online marketers are terrific people who are extremely generous with their time and talent.** They create products will make you money online, funnel traffic to your site, increase your SEO, and establish your site as a professional business with a high rate of customer satisfaction.

One more thing. DON'T get carried away by each and every opportunity I told you about. I would have to write hundreds of books like this to show **all the ways to make money online.** But whatever the niche is the basics still apply. As you learn more about making money online you can up-scale your site and product. You can do videos and upload them to Youtube. Do podcasts. Create Vlogs (video logs)

<u>But Just Not YET</u>.

As I said earlier the people who actually make money online are those who took the time to learn the process. Studied under those who were already successful and knew exactly how to make a website profitable. Eric Holmlund has an excellent free tutorial program on how to start an internet business, at http://ericstips.com and so does Affilorama

In addition you can always start simply by going back to the www.bummarketingmethod.com mentioned earlier and sell your affiliate product through article marketing, which won't cost you a cent.

So once you've selected a niche, and have created a Word Press website after purchasing a domain name, web hoster and auto-responder, or signed up with SBI, the next step is to join forums and interact with others in your niche. This is done for the same reason Wal-Mart watches what Target's doing who watches what Macys doing etc.

When I decided I wanted to be a writer full time, the first thing I did was join a writers group. There I discovered that most people are decent and are willing to help someone starting out to get a leg up.

One of the most helpful and useful forums is www.warriorforum.com It's free to join but if you want to become an affiliate for some of their products you'll have to join Warrior Plus.

It costs something like ten dollars for a lifetime membership and that's was only recently added to keep hackers and spammers out.

I don't have any business affiliate programs with the Warrior Forum but I am a member and it is perhaps the best place to go to get a real education on making money on line from people who do it on a regular basis.

What I find the most useful there is that experienced online marketers review the product sold on Warrior Plus and rate them for their value. And because these people ARE experienced, they cut right through the BS and can let you know right away if a product is worth buying.

So I suggest you join and spend some time there. Just not too much, remember you're a business owner now.

If you don't find any forums there that address your particular chosen niche, just go to google search and type it in. For example: If your niche is rare coin collection just type in rare coin collection forum and Google will give you a listing of several you can join and take part in.

Another advantage to joining forums is that you can get tips and advice that can help you with a particular problem or, more importantly, keep you from wasting time by setting up a site where the title keyword is ineffective or has little to no active searches.

There are many, many tricks of the trade and finding out what they are and how to effectively use them can be a big help when it comes to up scaling your site and getting more traffic.

Once you master the basics and can drive traffic to your site THEN I suggest you go to youtube and search for additional information from people like Vic Strizheus, Mike Long and Greg Morrison's http://www.omgmachines.com/ (join the free membership site for their videos, well worth it) and Pat Flynn's videos. They are very informative and you can learn quite a bit very quickly…

BUT…

___Just remember these people are professional internet marketers who sell high-end products!___

They have made MILLIONS online and the one thing they do very well is sell products and services.

And after watching their tutorials you will likely say to yourself, *"WOW! All I have to do is follow their system and I can become rich like them??!!"*

And the funny thing is, you probably can,

BUT JUST NOT YET!

Why? Because the one thing they *can't* teach you is **EXPERIENCE!**

And that is why a lot of new internet marketers fail. They fail because they jumped head-first into the big leagues before spending the time necessary in the minor leagues to learn the finer points of the game.

Neither Vic, Mike, Greg nor Pat became rich overnight. They spent several years working hard to become the wealthy professionals they are today, learning their craft, listening to those more experienced, and most of all getting a real feel for the industry.

People learn at different speeds. You may have a natural talent for this and be making $3000 a week in six months. For others it may take a year or two to start making the big money.

My advice? Take the time to learn HOW to make money online. Take baby steps and master the basics. Then build a solid business foundation. As you become more experienced, you will see opportunities in your niche that you hadn't realized earlier and how those opportunities can up-scale and benefit your business.

Personally I have spent thousand over the years on product upgrades and services and almost every one of them benefited my business in some way

The only purchases I made that I regretted were the one that I bought that promised specular results but required specific knowledge and skills I didn't realize I still needed to learn. In my case they were SEO and back linking programs as well as anchor text methodology.

The price of an education, right?

Publicity and Advertising:
Keep in mind that **although your making money online venture is on the internet, the brick and mortar rules of business still apply.** Meaning if you want customers, you have to get your business out and in front of the buying public.

One little trick you can use to get online buyers to give you a look, is to use the same keywords people looking to buy use.
For example: Say your niche is dollhouses. On your website include keywords like: best dollhouse prices, top selling dollhouses, best rated dollhouses, most popular dollhouses, dollhouses for sale, etc.

When people are looking to buy a specific product they get right to the point. They want to buy a product, NOW. So make sure you are right there in the forefront when they hit that google search button by rigging the keywords so that they are the very same as those used by the buyers.

Also, and this is especially important as an online marketer, always OVER supply! Always give a little extra with each sale.

Why is this important? Because with Brick and Mortar stores the customer meets with the seller face to face. The buyer gets to look them up and down and can decide right then and there is they want to do business with that person.

How many time have you walked into a store to buy something and were immediately put off by the sleazy appearance and pushy persona of the sales person? Or on the other side, were immediately impressed and comfortable with the store and its employees?

Online, your customer doesn't have that option, they don't know who you are, what you really look like or whether you can be trusted. So the only way you can build a rapport with them is to OVER DELIVER!

This way they will be pleasantly surprised and it's human nature to want to reciprocate.

So they tell their friends and they tell **their** friends and if you keep up the good work in a relatively short period of time you will have amassed a loyal following and will be making money online.

And of course there is the good old fashion advertisement. Should you decide to become an affiliate for online services like aweber.com namecheap.com or hostgator.com They offer banners with your affiliate link that you can place on your site and should someone click and purchase through your link you get the commission.

Another way is to advertise your product on Google's adwords.com through a pay per click called PPC or pay for impressions called PPM campaign.
Here's how they works.

For Pay Per Click: You find a product, become an affiliate, set up an opt-in/squeeze page and link to your auto-responder. You then sign up for an account on Google AdWords and bid on how much you want to spend when a person clicks on your Advertisement link

Say the average bid for your product is $0.17 per click. So you bid $0.18 per click to beat out your competition. What you are doing is paying Google 18 cents every time someone clicks on your advert and hopefully gives you their name and email address so they can see the full sales presentation of your product and buy it.

Keep in mind that although many people will click, only a small percentage will opt-in. BUT! The ones that do are people who are actually looking to buy a product like yours so by having them on your email list gives you the opportunity to contact them each time you have something for sale that is similar to what they originally clicked to see.

Don't be spammy! These people are trusting you with their email address and will unsubscribe if you waste their time pitching products they have no interest in.

FIRST NOTE and this is VERY IMPORTANT. When you set up your first AdWords campaign MAKE SURE YOU CONTACT THEM AND TELL THEM **YOU DO NOT WANT THEM TO ADD MONEY TO THE CAMPAIGN WITHOUT YOUR DIRECT PERMISSION**!

At the time of my first AdWords campaign I did not know this and didn't realize that AdWords default program takes money from your debit or credit card to replace the money spent on clicks.

I wound up owing them $120.00 before I realized what was happening SO, although this is a good way to start collecting buyers, KEEP A CLOSE EYE ON EXPENIDURES!

The next option is Pay Per Impressions (PPM). This means pay per <u>one-thousand</u> impressions.

Instead of only paying for clicks to your advert, with PPM they place your advert on thousands of websites but you pay whether customer clicks on it or not. You're paying for the placement not the click or the opt-in.

Since I sell books, paying for impressions or clicks is not cost effective for me but, I suggest you view a few videos on the topic on youtube. See which, if any, is advantageous to your business.

There are a lot of ways to make your product available to the public, the important thing is to find out which methods get the most bang for the buck.

The CPA method:

As I mentioned in the beginning of this book there are hundreds of ways to make money online but perhaps the

most popular is the CPA method also known as Click per Action
Here's how it works:
You go to a CPA site like www.odigger.com or www.offervault.com and select a product in your niche. Take for example Health and Diet. So you pick a product like Joint Pain Relief supplement which comes with an opt-in page that offers a free bottle just for putting in their name, email and home address. And once they do, you get a commission of about $40.00 per sign up.
<u>The best thing is you don't have to sell them anything!</u> For you to get paid all they have to do is send for the free bottle.

There are also offers that don't even require a name and email address, Just their ZIPCODE!! Of course you don't get anywhere near $40 for a sign up but for commission of say only $5 a zip-code, that could add up to a nice piece of change at the end of the month.

Even better if you roll out a few of them!

Before I bring this to a close I want to give you a list of the things to do in order to become successful and make money online.
These tips come directly for Alex Becker of http://source-wave.com and http://omgmachines.com

1) **Start by improving yourself.**
   No matter HOW good you are you can always get better. So start looking for ways to increase your knowledge, for ways to better use your time, for ways to get yourself in front of more people, for ways to better close a business deal and finally for ways to become the best at what you are doing.

2) **When you decide on a niche learn everything there is to know about it.**
   You do this by finding and following the people who are in the same niche, and who are already successful at it. Then you befriend them by offering to help them, by buying their products and then by learning all you can.

3) **Focus on learning the basics**
   This is essential. You can't create a multi-million dollar empire in the dog training niche if you don't know anything about dogs and the same goes for any niche. Create a strong foundation so as your business expands it will continue to do well.

4) **Take Action!**
   Don't wait until everything is perfect. The best way to become good at something is to begin DOING IT. Once you have your site up and running, start

advertising, start selling, start making friends and start learning how to create your own products.

5) Risk Failure!
Those who succeed are those who get out of their comfort zone and take chances. Find the people who want what you have to sell and try to convince them to buy it. As noted earlier you can find these people by searching Facebook and other sources.

6) Get out in front of people.
Offer to teach people about your niche. For example, each year there is a book fair where authors gather to sell their books and talk with other authors. And each year I offer to be one of the featured speakers and spend an hour explaining the fine points of writing and publishing and in return for giving me their names and emails, I give them a free copy of my book How to Write, Publish

& Market your Novel into a Best-Seller.

So that's it, friend. You now have all you need to BEGIN making money online. As stated throughout this book there is no special formula, no secret money-making scheme, no get-rich-quick software, no set-it and forget it business plan…

Making money online is the same as making money in any venture. You start small and scale up as your KNOWLEDGE and UNDERSTANDING of you niche increases.

Work very hard and always remember that **you do not stop when you are tired, you stop when you are done!**

As one of my mentors Brian G. Johnson of Marketing Easy Street always says. "People don't fail at making money online, they simply quit before success can happen.

Se lets' do one final review of some of the online marketing information. I put it here not to be used right now. (especially if you're just getting started) but as a place to go once your skills and traffic start picking up speed and you're looking to go to the next step.

For example this is an excellent site for instruction on How to Open an Internet Store. http://www.smallbusinesscomputing.com/e marketing/article.php/3601376/Starting-An-Online-Store-The-Essential-Checklist--Part-I.html

(these processes and tools will become necessary once you are selling a lot of products from your site regularly.)

As your making money online skills increase you will discover that your "Flying by the seat of your pants" days are over and it's time to become a full-fledged and respected member of the business community

So go out there and become healthy, wealthy and wise in the world of online marketing!

Made in the USA
Charleston, SC
26 October 2014